THE FRUITS WE EAT

BY GAIL GIBBONS

Holiday House / New York

To Shania, Denise, and Shane Thurston

Special thanks to Becky Sideman, Horticultural Specialist at the University of New Hampshire, Durham, New Hampshire.

Printed and Bound in September 2021
at Toppan Leefung, DongGuan City, China.
www.holidayhouse.com

7 9 10 8

Library of Congress Cataloging-in-Publication Data
Gibbons, Gail.
The fruits we eat / by Gail Gibbons. – First edition.
pages cm
Audience: 4-8
ISBN 978-0-8234-3204-2 (hardcover)
1. Fruit–Juvenile literature. I. Title.
SB357.2.G53 2015
634—dc23
2014007379
ISBN 978-0-8234-3571-5 (paperback)

ORANGES

APPLES

PES

PEARS

PEACHES

CA

Most fruits are PERENNIALS. They grow over and over again throughout many seasons.

ANNUAL FRUITS grow for only one season. Then they must be planted again.

Usually fruits have a fleshy texture.

BERR

Look at the many kinds of fruits. We eat parts of a fruit or the entire fruit.

MyPLATE

Recommendations for eating a well-balanced diet on a day-to-day basis

FRUITS	GRAINS
VEGETABLES	PROTEIN

DAIRY

www.choosemyplate.gov
USDA: United States Department of Agriculture

Fruits taste good. They help keep our bodies healthy and strong.

Every child should try to eat between 1 and 1½ cups (236.6 and 354.9 ml) of fruit each day.

Fruits are eaten in different ways.

5

PLANTS, BUSHES, VINES, AND...

PLANTS

STRAWBERRIES

A BOTANIST is a scientist who studies plants.

BUSHES

BLUEBERRIES

VINES

CANTALOUPES

GRAPES

Fruits begin as blossoms. POLLINATION happens when a grain of pollen from a stamen lands on the stigma of another same kind of blossom.

STIGMA

STAMEN

The flowers get pollinated and fall off, and then the fruits begin to grow.

Botanists group fruits according to the types of vegetation they grow on.

TREES

CORTLAND APPLE TREE

BARTLETT PEAR TREE

RELIANCE PEACH TREE

NAVEL ORANGE TREE

Many fruits taste sweet. Others can taste tart.

PLANTS AND ...

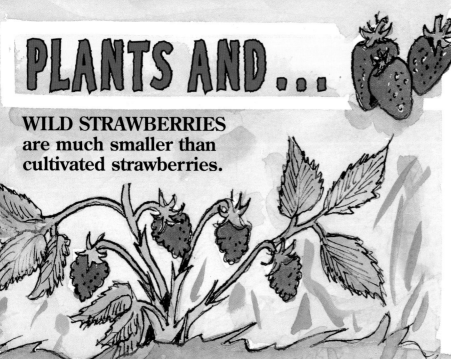

WILD STRAWBERRIES are much smaller than cultivated strawberries.

STRAWBERRIES grow on a plant.

All berries are **PERENNIALS**.

Almost all berries that we eat are **CULTIVATED** (CUL-tuh-vayt-ed). That means people grow and care for them until harvesttime.

THE PARTS OF A STRAWBERRY

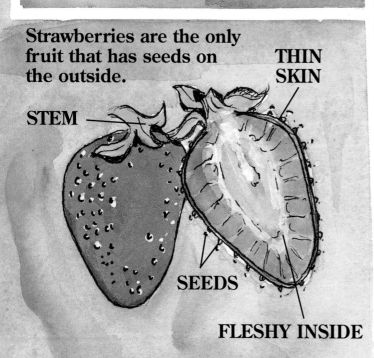

Strawberries are the only fruit that has seeds on the outside.

THIN SKIN

STEM

SEEDS

FLESHY INSIDE

HARVESTTIME is when the fruits are picked.

Strawberries taste sweet.

Berries are small fruits. They can be soft or hard. Some berries taste sweet. Others taste tart.

BUSHES

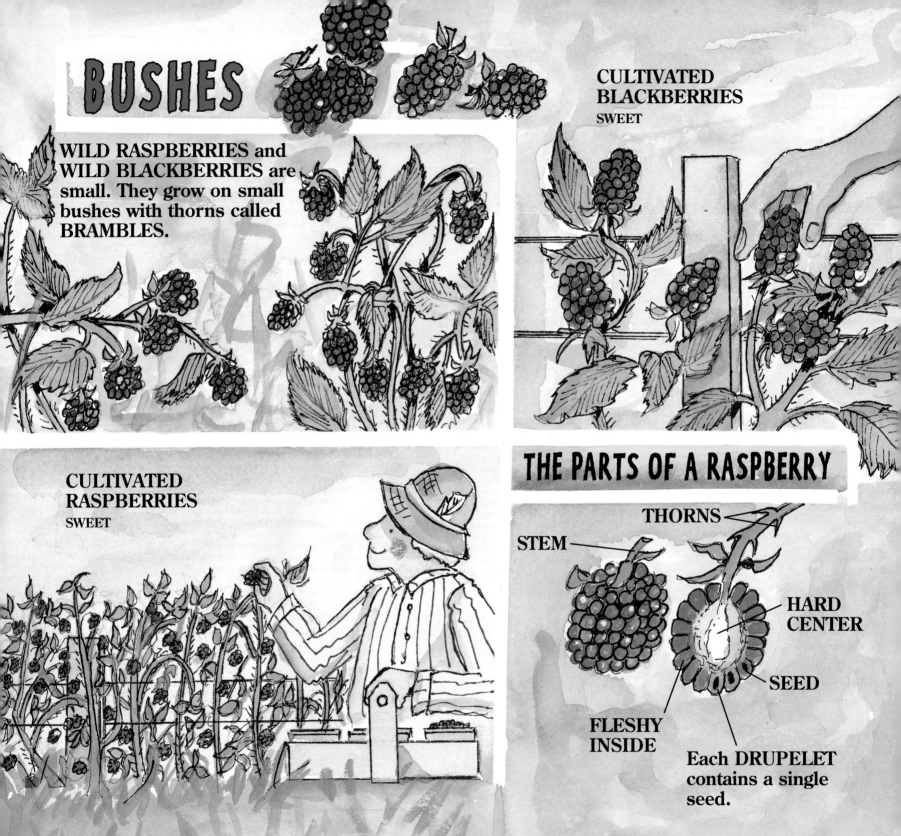

WILD RASPBERRIES and WILD BLACKBERRIES are small. They grow on small bushes with thorns called BRAMBLES.

CULTIVATED BLACKBERRIES
SWEET

CULTIVATED RASPBERRIES
SWEET

THE PARTS OF A RASPBERRY

THORNS

STEM

HARD CENTER

SEED

FLESHY INSIDE

Each DRUPELET contains a single seed.

Other berries grow on bushes. Some of them are made up of clusters of small, smooth-skinned, ball-like shapes called drupelets.

WILD BLUEBERRIES are small. Most of them grow on bushes that are low to the ground.

SWEET

CULTIVATED BLUEBERRIES are large. They grow on tall bushes.

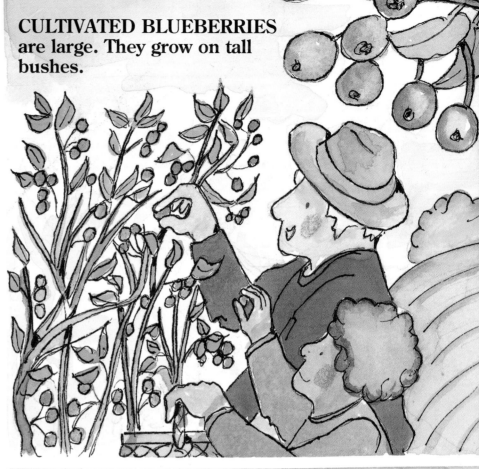

THE PARTS OF A BLUEBERRY

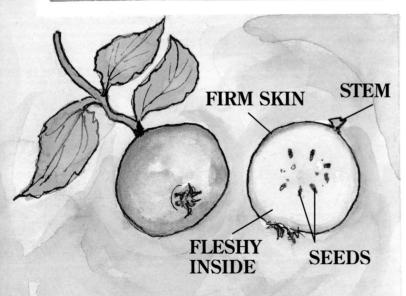

FIRM SKIN
STEM
FLESHY INSIDE
SEEDS

Smooth berries contain one or more seeds.

CRANBERRIES
TART

GOOSEBERRIES
TART

CURRANTS
TART

Many berries we eat are smooth.

PINEAPPLE PLANT

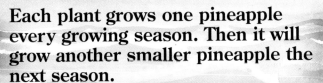

Each plant grows one pineapple every growing season. Then it will grow another smaller pineapple the next season.

Pineapples grow in warm climates.

Growers cut SHOOTS from the bottoms of mature pineapple plants.

When a shoot is planted, a new, big, juicy pineapple will grow the next season.

THE PARTS OF A PINEAPPLE

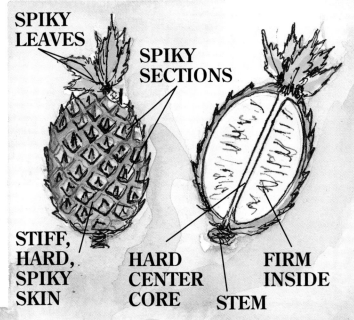

SPIKY LEAVES

SPIKY SECTIONS

STIFF, HARD, SPIKY SKIN

HARD CENTER CORE

STEM

FIRM INSIDE

Pineapples are perennials. They are large and thorny members of the berry family. Once spiky outsides are cut off, the sweet, juicy pineapple fruits can be eaten.

A BANANA PLANT

Growers cut SHOOTS from the bottoms of mature banana plants.

When a shoot is planted, another banana plant will grow.

A BANANA PLANT can grow to be 15 feet (4.6 meters) to 20 feet (6.1 meters) tall.

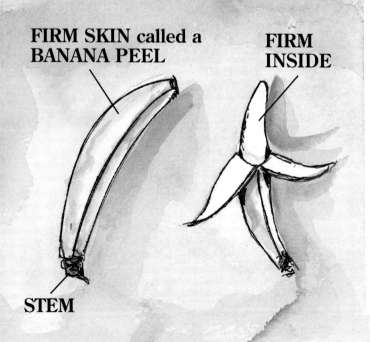

A BUNCH OF BANANAS

Bananas grow in warm climates.

THE PARTS OF A BANANA

FIRM SKIN called a BANANA PEEL

FIRM INSIDE

STEM

Some varieties of bananas are called PLANTAINS.

They must be cooked before eating.

Bananas are sweet and full of nutrition. A banana plant is an annual that grows quickly and produces only one crop in its lifetime.

VINE FRUITS

At the beginning of a growing season, seeds must be planted. Growers plant the seeds in small mounds of dirt.

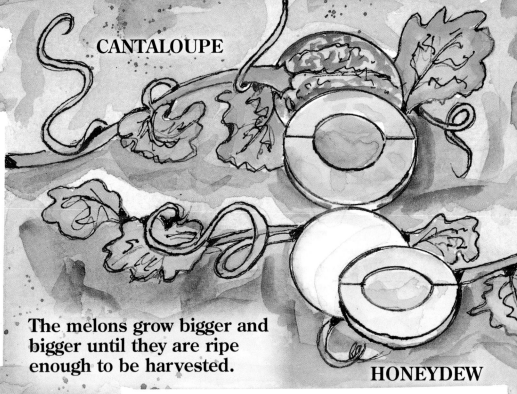

CANTALOUPE

The melons grow bigger and bigger until they are ripe enough to be harvested.

HONEYDEW

Melons are grown in the summer or in warm climates.

Most WATERMELONS grow to be long and round.

THE PARTS OF A WATERMELON

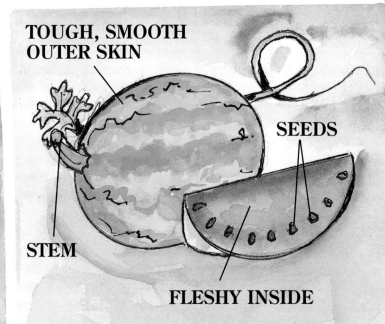

TOUGH, SMOOTH OUTER SKIN

SEEDS

STEM

FLESHY INSIDE

Melons grow on vines that creep along the ground. They taste sweet and are annuals.

Before growing season begins growers prune, meaning they cut back, the vines so more grapes will grow.

PRUNING SHEARS

GLOVES

Grapes grow in CLUSTERS.

GOLDEN MUSCAT GRAPES SWEET

FENCE

THE PARTS OF A GRAPE

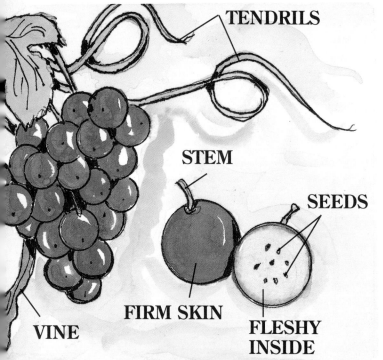

TENDRILS

STEM

SEEDS

FIRM SKIN

FLESHY INSIDE

VINE

Grapes grow on grapevines in clusters. They are perennial fruits. Many grapes are round, and others are oval in shape. Some grapes taste sweet, others taste tart.

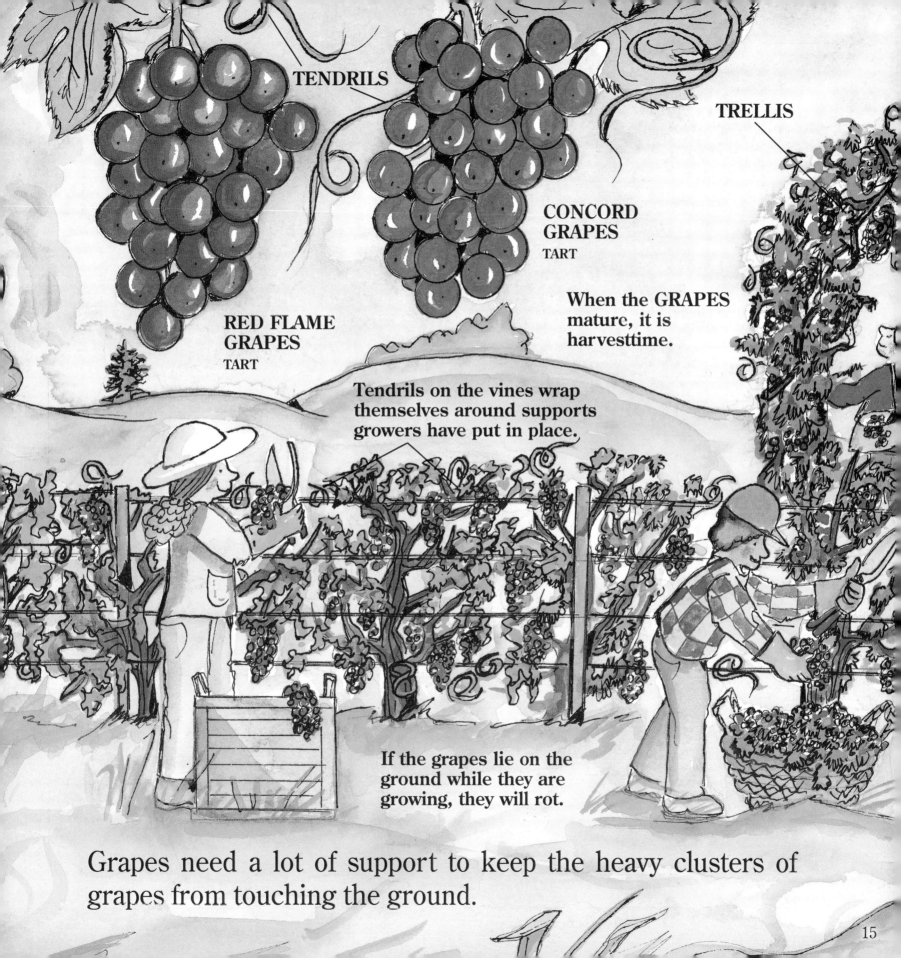

TENDRILS

TRELLIS

CONCORD
GRAPES
TART

RED FLAME
GRAPES
TART

When the GRAPES mature, it is harvesttime.

Tendrils on the vines wrap themselves around supports growers have put in place.

If the grapes lie on the ground while they are growing, they will rot.

Grapes need a lot of support to keep the heavy clusters of grapes from touching the ground.

FRUIT TREES

AN APPLE TREE

All fruit trees are PERENNIALS.

GOLDEN DELICIOUS
SWEET

GRANNY SMITH
TART

THE PARTS OF AN APPLE

STEM THIN SKIN
CRISPY INSIDE

SEEDS
CORE

SEEDS are in CHAMBERS called CARPELS.

MCINTOSH
SWEET

Apples can taste sweet or tart.

Throughout an apple-growing season the apples in the orchard have grown bigger. When the apples ripen, it's harvesttime.

A PEAR TREE

BARTLETT PEAR

BOSC PEAR

SECKEL PEAR

THE PARTS OF A PEAR

STEM

THIN SKIN

CORE

JUICY INSIDE

SMALL SEEDS

Pears are very sweet and juicy when they are ripe.

A CHERRY TREE

THE PARTS OF A CHERRY

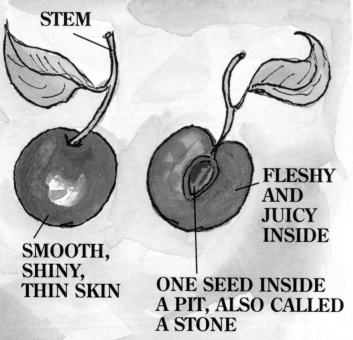

STEM

SMOOTH, SHINY, THIN SKIN

ONE SEED INSIDE A PIT, ALSO CALLED A STONE

FLESHY AND JUICY INSIDE

BING CHERRIES
SWEET

MONTMORENCY CHERRIES
TART

ROYAL ANN CHERRIES
SWEET

Cherries are a small fruit. Many taste sweet. Others taste tart. They are picked when they ripen and are colorful.

A PEACH TREE

RELIANCE
PEACH

MAY GOLD
PEACH

THE PARTS OF A PEACH

THIN, FUZZY
SKIN

STEM

FLESHY AND
JUICY INSIDE

ONE SEED INSIDE
A PIT, ALSO CALLED
A STONE

Peaches are juicy and sweet. The skin of a peach is fuzzy.

LEMON AND LIME TREES

MEYER LEMONS

Lemons and limes taste sour and tart.

EUREKA LEMONS

THE PARTS OF A LEMON

STEM

SEEDS

PULPY FLESH

Tough skin called RIND

SECTIONS OF A LEMON

KEY LIMES

These trees grow tart citrus fruits. Lemons and limes are harvested when they become ripe.

ORANGE AND GRAPEFRUIT TREES

VALENCIA ORANGES

NAVEL ORANGES

MARSH GRAPEFRUIT
TART

RUBY GRAPEFRUIT
SWEET

THE PARTS OF AN ORANGE

STEM

SECTIONS OF AN ORANGE

RIND

PULPY FLESH

SEEDS

Other citrus trees grow juicy oranges and grapefruits. Oranges taste sweet. Some grapefruits taste sweet, others taste tart.

Hardy fruits grow in SEASONAL CLIMATES, where the weather changes throughout the year, creating seasons.

Many bushes, vines, and fruit trees become DORMANT during the winter.

DORMANT means alive but not growing. This happens where winters are cold.

Fruits are grown in different climates. There are seasonal climates.

A MACHETE is used to cut the thick plant stalks.

FRAGILE!

There are warm climates.

23

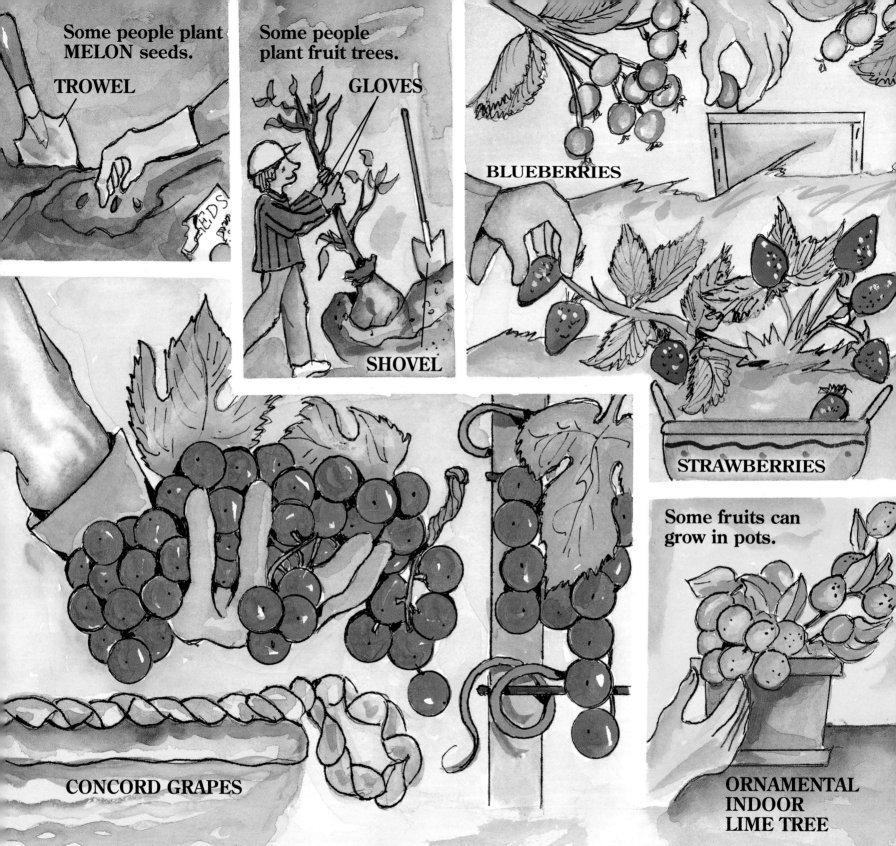

Some people plant MELON seeds.

TROWEL

Some people plant fruit trees.

GLOVES

SHOVEL

BLUEBERRIES

STRAWBERRIES

Some fruits can grow in pots.

CONCORD GRAPES

ORNAMENTAL INDOOR LIME TREE

Many people enjoy growing their own fruits. They must choose the fruits that can grow in the climates where they live.

Most of the fruits we eat are grown on large industrial farms.

HARVESTING ON A LARGE FRUIT FARM

HARVESTING STRAWBERRIES

HARVESTING CRANBERRIES

CRANBERRY HARVESTER

HARVESTING BANANAS

MACHETE

HARVESTING GRAPES

BASKETS

During harvesting, the fruits must be handled carefully.

On large fruit farms, many people do the harvesting.
There are so many fruits!

The fruits will be sorted and washed. Some will be packed whole. The rest will go to different fruit-processing centers.

The fresh fruits and the processed foods are shipped and delivered to stores near and far away.

Some small fruit growers sell what they grow at farm stands.

FROZEN FRUITS, CANNED FRUITS, and many other fruit products

SALE

FRESH FRUITS

Most people buy fresh fruits and fruit products in stores. The fruit displays are so colorful!

OTHER FRUITS WE EAT

KIWIS

AVOCADO

MANGO

PAPAYA

DATES

PLUMS

PERSIMMONS

OLIVES

APRICOTS

FIGS

TANGERINES

STAR
FRUITS

POMEGRANATES

FRUITS...FRUITS...FRUITS...

Many fruits we eat are seedless. Over time different fruits were altered, or changed, to become seedless.

Watermelons contain about 92 percent water.

Most fruits are harvested by hand.

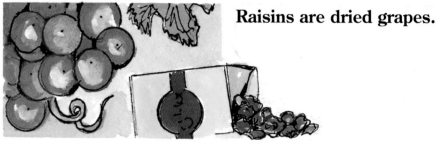

Raisins are dried grapes.

WASHINGTON

The state of Washington produces about 70 percent of the apples consumed in the United States.

Washington, DC is famous for its cherry blossoms that bloom in the spring.

ONTARIO

The province of Ontario is the largest apple-producing province in Canada.

A coconut is classified as a fruit. A tomato is classified as a fruit vegetable.

CENTRAL AMERICA

SOUTH AMERICA

Most bananas we eat in the United States are shipped to us from warm climates.

WEBSITES

In the USA:
www.choosemyplate.gov/
food-groups/
click on: Fruits

In Canada:
www.hc-sc.gc.ca
click on: Canada's
Food Guide